MY THEOLOGY

THE WORD WITHIN THE WORDS

Other titles in the MY THEOLOGY series

Duppy Conqueror
Robert Beckford

The Primacy of Love
Ilia Delio

Return from a Distant Country
Alister McGrath

MY THEOLOGY

MALCOLM GUITE

THE WORD WITHIN THE WORDS

DARTON·LONGMAN+TODD

First published in 2021 by
Darton, Longman and Todd Ltd
1 Spencer Court
140 – 142 Wandsworth High Street
London SW18 4JJ

© 2021 Malcolm Guite

The right of Malcolm Guite to be identified as the Author of this work has been asserted in accordance with the Copyright, Designs and patents Act 1988.

ISBN: 978-1-913657-38-3

A catalogue record for this book is available from the British Library.

Printed and bound in Great Britain by
Bell & Bain, Glasgow

For Judith Tonry, friend and amanuensis

Contents

Acknowledgements   9
Introduction   11

1. Scripture: The Word beneath the words   23
2. Liturgy: The Word between the words   41
3. Sacrament: The Word transforms the world   59

Conclusion: Christ alive and loose in the world   81

Acknowledgements

MANY PEOPLE HAVE contributed to the making of this little book, both those who helped me lay the groundwork of my theology itself and those who have helped me in the task of setting it out in these pages. I would like to acknowledge the crucial insight and guidance of the Fr Warren Tanghe, who was chaplain in my undergraduate days at Pembroke and about whom I have written in chapter three, and who prepared me for confirmation. Dr Jeremy Begbie, who taught me doctrine at theological college, and has remained a friend and mentor, has also played a large part in the shaping of my theology. My wife Maggie has been a constant companion in faith as in life and her example and preaching as well as her steadfast love have helped to make and shape my theology as well as my life. My friend and PA Philippa Pearson has, as always, helped me stay organised and more or less on top of my many tasks and obligations, and finally Judith Tonry, another friend and fellow Christian, to whom this book is dedicated, kindly acted as an amanuensis and conversation partner throughout the making of this book. I am grateful to all of them, as to others too numerous to mention, not least my many students whose sharp questions have in turn sharpened my thinking.

Introduction

I MUST BEGIN with a paradox. I am to write a book entitled *My Theology* and yet in the deepest sense, my Christian faith, and the theology to which it gives rise, is not strictly speaking *mine*, but something given, something willingly received, treasured and responded to. The *response* is mine, but the faith itself is a sheer gift, something neither I, nor all of humanity, could have imagined for ourselves, but a mystery, revealed uniquely in the coming of Christ, in his Incarnation, Death and Resurrection, a mystery which calls forth and kindles our deepest responses. That response summons both our powers of reason and imagination, for both are necessary if we are to begin to explore and understand our faith. For, in the end, that is what theology is, as Anselm beautifully put it: *Fides Quaerens Intellectum* – faith seeking understanding. So the faith is given and some of the response is inherited, and yet to be a true response it must also be personal and it is that personal response which I offer here as 'my theology'. In the seventeenth century, Sir Thomas Browne[1], a medical doctor, wrote his wonderful essay *Religio Medici* – the religion of a doctor. What I offer here might be termed a *Religio Poetae* – the Faith of a Poet. My vocation as a poet attunes me particularly to the mysteries and beauties of language: the magic of words, the cadences and music of speech, but most of all, kindling and glimmering through all the words we use, the mystery of meaning itself and the wonderful vehicle of metaphor whereby one thing can be transfigured by the meaning of another.

But what is that faith, to which I can give my personal response – 'my theology'? Well, of course, we might find it already set out in any of the four gospels, or analysed and expressed in golden passages in the letters of St. Paul.

---

[1] Sir Thomas Browne, polymath and author, 19 October 1605 – 19 October 1682.

INTRODUCTION

We might find it beautifully summarised and gathered together in the Creed, we might find it shaped, expressed and sung in that interactive poem, which is the church's liturgy, and especially in the sacrament of the eucharist. We might find that it shines most clearly to us in the lives of the saints, living and departed. Any of these living sources of faith might be the starting point for our journey. I expect that for most people who 'profess and call themselves Christian' there is, amongst all these interwoven texts and traditions, one particular strand that calls and draws them more than others, and helps to make sense of all the rest. Given what I have already said about poetry and language it is, for me, the opening words of the Gospel of St John:

> In the beginning was the Word, and the Word was with God, and the Word was God. He was in the beginning with God. All things came into being through him, and without him not one thing came into being. [2]

[2] John 1:1–5 (NRSV).

The heart of any poet would leap to find that in this mysterious account of God himself, and of his primal act of creation, the Word, the *Logos* or essence of all meaning, has a central place. For a poet, all words have a magical, generative power. They exist in themselves before the creation of a poem and it is in, and through, and out of them that the poem comes into being. This opening passage of John's Gospel offers us the encouraging and utterly transformative idea that we ourselves are a poem, that there is a poet behind the world, who not only speaks that world into being but speaks us into it, so that we might behold its glory and respond ourselves with poems spoken back to the maker. And John's Gospel, as these opening words make clear, is riffing on Genesis, and the opening of the whole Bible itself. For there in that *In Principio*, in that 'in the beginning', we see God speaking the cosmos into existence by the sheer Fiat of his word *'Let there be light; and there was light.'*[3] Furthermore, Genesis goes on

---

[3] Genesis 1:3 (NRSV): Then God said, *'Let there be light'; and there was light.*

INTRODUCTION

to tell us that when he speaks us into being, we are made in his image, made to be makers, that our words too will have weight and meaning, as we see in that mysterious passage where God brings the animals to Adam to see what he would name them.

This idea, that I myself might be part of a poem, then even as I speak and breathe, I am being breathed and spoken into being, had a profound effect on me and is right at the core of my faith and theology. I tried to express it once in a poem of my own, on 'O Sapienta' the great 'O' Antiphon that calls on Christ as wisdom:

> O Wisdom, coming forth from the mouth
>   of the Most High,
> reaching from one end to the other,
> mightily and sweetly ordering all things:
> Come and teach us the way of prudence. [4]

Here is my poem responding to that antiphon:

[4] *O Sapentia* the first of 'The Great Os', the *Magnificat* antiphons used at Vespers in the last seven days of Advent.

O Sapientia

I cannot think unless I have been thought,
Nor can I speak unless I have been spoken;
I cannot teach except as I am taught,
Or break the bread except as I am broken.
O Mind behind the mind through which
    I seek,
O Light within the light by which I see,
O Word beneath the words with which
    I speak,
O founding, unfound Wisdom, finding me,
O sounding Song whose depth is sounding
    me,
O Memory of time, reminding me,
My Ground of Being, always grounding me,
My Maker's bounding line, defining me:
Come, hidden Wisdom, come with all you
    bring,
Come to me now, disguised as everything. [5]

But the prologue to John's Gospel goes even further than this. In the fourteenth verse comes

---

[5] *Waiting on the Word*, Malcolm Guite (Canterbury Press, 2015), p. 66.

INTRODUCTION

that extraordinary turn which brings us down from the heights of Greek philosophy, down from the heavens and into this solid world of flesh and blood, into the heart of our own humanity and into the very core of Christianity:

> And the Word became flesh and lived among us, and we have seen his glory, the glory as of a father's only son, full of grace and truth. [6]

This is simply astonishing. All the great philosophers in the Western tradition (and indeed in the East) up to this point had been trying to get us *out of* the flesh, not *into* it. If they believed there was a single *Logos*, a transcendent and eternal being, the source of goodness, truth and beauty, then their aim was to leave this world of little *logoi*, the myriad of little words and things, and to return, purged of time, purged of multiplicity, back into that single, undifferentiated, eternal *Logos*: so

---

[6] John 1:14 (NRSV).

Plato and many after him believed. Then comes this gospel, and turns everything around.

And so, in John 1:14, we see how God's Love comes down, gets stuck in, gets involved. Not only in the messy business of our living, but in the bloody business of our dying.

And this too, this miracle and mystery of Incarnation, has rich parallels with poetry itself. Perhaps the greatest passage in English about what poetry is and how it works comes in Shakespeare's famous description of the poet in *A Midsummer Night's Dream*:

> The poet's eye, in fine frenzy rolling,
> Doth glance from heaven to earth,
>   from earth to heaven;
> And as imagination bodies forth
> The forms of things unknown,
>   the poet's pen
> Turns them to shapes and gives to
>   airy nothing
> A local habitation and a name.[7]

[7] *A Midsummer Night's Dream*, William Shakespeare, *c.* 1595.

INTRODUCTION

I used to read this as simply and only an account of poetry: how poetry must include both heaven and earth, both the invisible and the visible, the things we scarcely apprehend and the things we know and comprehend, how poetry must not only include, but must ultimately connect these two things: must woo the invisible into visibility, must make a beautiful bower or 'habitation' for our fleeting apprehensions, so that they can come home to us and begin to be comprehended. Poetry must also take the visible things, the things of earth, the things we think we comprehend and open them out to the heavenly, so that the familiar is for a moment transfigured and the earth, disenchanted by our dull habits, might be re-enchanted again until we see that the earth, like the heavens, is full of the glory of God. How does poetry achieve this? It is all there, at the heart of this passage, in Shakespeare's brilliant juxtaposition of the two words *imagination* and *bodies:*

> And as imagination bodies forth
> The forms of things unknown,
>   the poet's pen
> Turns them to shapes

The poet is not content with a flimsy 'imaginary' insubstantial or merely wordy realm, but strives constantly to body things forth. To show us real flesh and blood, to make of the poem a visible, approachable, local habitation in which we can at last, see the invisible and give a name to those loves and apprehensions which give life meaning.

But it was only when I came to re-read this passage in light of the Prologue to John's Gospel, that I realised that, as well as describing his own art as a poet, Shakespeare was echoing John's account of the art of the Divine Poet. It is all there: the gap between heaven and earth, the need for a connection, and then the moment of bodying forth: the Word is made flesh and then that flesh is made available for us to see, is given a local habitation and best of all a name: the holy name

INTRODUCTION

of Jesus. The first question of the disciples to Jesus in John's Gospel is 'where are you staying'[8] or as Shakespeare would have known it in the Vulgate *Magister, ubi habitat* – where is your habitation. In Jesus Christ heaven itself is bodied forth, given a local habitation and a name.

Everything else follows from this, certainly everything else in 'my theology'. Everything in this book, about the scriptures, the liturgy and the sacraments and about the risen Christ, free and loose in the World, free to encounter us anywhere, everywhere and in anyone, all stems from this one continuous miracle and mystery: his Incarnation.

---

[8] John 1:38 (NRSV). *When Jesus turned and saw them following, he said to them, 'What are you looking for?' They said to him, 'Rabbi' (which translated means Teacher), 'where are you staying?'*

1

Scripture: The Word beneath the words

I CANNOT OVERSTATE the importance of the Bible, not only for the formation and expression of my own faith and the theology I am sharing here, but also for the formation of all of us: our minds, our lives, our culture and our very language. Among the many blessings of belonging to a faith which has such an important place for written scriptures, is the blessing of literacy and literary culture. It is a simple fact that the desire to read and share the Bible, translated into our own language, has been the main driver for literacy and everything that pertains to it: from the production of paper and the invention of printing, to children learning their letters in elementary schools. And yet, there is a paradox here. Important as the scriptures are, their true importance lies in something beyond their pages: it is not the many authors of the Bible, but the one God to whom their writings point, that make the scriptures holy. Martin Luther put this very beautifully in the introduction to his Old Testament translation:

> Here you will find the swaddling–clothes and the mangers in which Christ lies, and to which the angel points the shepherds. Simple and little are the swaddling–clothes, but dear is the treasure, Christ, that lies in them.[9]

Luther's distinction between the scriptures as words that bring us to Christ, and Christ himself as the true Word of God, the Word, within and beneath the Words of the Bible, is vital because sometimes the Bible is misused and misunderstood. Instead of turning its pages to unveil the love of God shining out at us from the face of Christ, just as the shepherds might have moved aside the swaddling bands to

[9] Martin Luther, the introduction to his Old Testament translation of 1545.

SCRIPTURE: THE WORD BENEATH THE WORDS

reveal the child they contain, instead we empty the precious sheets of the Christ-child, and start ruffling through them for all kinds of other things which are not part of their purpose, for which they were not given. Some people want to treat the Bible as though it were an A level science textbook dropped from heaven, others as though it were no more than a weighty legal compendium, complete with handy proof-texts for bringing others to book. For some scholars, worthy though they may be, the Bible seems to be little more than a vast archaeological dig, full of gaping holes and neatly piled and labelled shards full of 'Ur' texts. For others, this richly poetic, resonant and mysterious library of ancient wisdom has been reduced to a flat single line like the tickertape news-feed you see scrolling along the bottom of a television screen, as though all the Bible could show you was a stream of un-interpreted facts: what you would have seen for yourself if you had been stood there with a Camcorder.

Take, for example, the archetypal story of Noah's Ark. On the one hand we have a group of ardent literalists arguing with each other about cubits and gopher wood, and about the vexed question of whether dinosaurs and even unicorns found room on the Ark. On the other hand, we have earnest biblical scholars, making learned comparisons with other flood stories of the ancient Near-East and concerning themselves with the hypothetical editors and proto-redactors of the disassembled bricolage of the Genesis text. Neither of these groups seems to allow the story, as a story in itself, to give us what it has to offer, to tell us about who we really are and how we might live, to say something like this:

> We are all in the same boat, we have been gathered and saved into a community in which everyone, male and female, and even every species is important to God. We have been saved by the loving kindness and forethought of another, and the floods that seem to overwhelm us need not be our end of the story. There is a new beginning on offer, there is a new

covenant not only for us, but for the whole of creation, and over our redemption God sets the sign of his promise, the shimmering rainbow.

Perhaps the little children who have been putting rainbows in their windows throughout the coronavirus crisis understand Genesis better that either the fundamentalists or the scholars. For the early Church, of course, seeking Christ, the Word of God, amidst all the words in the Bible, and finding him in the Old Testament as well as the New, came naturally. Even the Ark itself was an archetype of the Cross: that piece of wood on which we were all lifted up above the floods of death, even as Christ was raised upon it that he might draw all of humanity on himself.

Indeed, there is a deeper sense in which the New Testament is a beautiful, radical re-reading of the Old Testament, as Richard Hays demonstrates in his brilliant book *Reading Backwards*.[10] And for all Christians, the

[10] *Reading Backwards: Figural Christology and the Fourfold Gospel Witness*, Richard Hays (SPCK, 2015).

absolute paradigm for understanding the Old Testament and indeed all the scriptures more widely, is the story of the Road to Emmaus. We think of those forlorn and confused disciples trying to understand the tragic events of Good Friday in the light of the scriptures as they thought they knew them. Many scriptures seemed to point to the idea that God blesses the righteous with success, that God 'will not suffer his Holy One to see corruption',[11] that the Messiah will triumph over earthly authorities and sit on David's throne and that the particular horror of crucifixion was reserved only for those who were utterly accursed by God. No wonder they thought that they had backed the wrong horse, and the disaster of Good Friday had proved Christ's claims to be false. It is all there in the tenses of Luke's narrative:

> Now on that same day two of them were going to a village called Emmaus, about

[11] Psalm 16:10 (KJV).

SCRIPTURE: THE WORD BENEATH THE WORDS

seven miles from Jerusalem, and talking with each other about all these things that had happened. While they were talking and discussing, Jesus himself came near and went with them, but their eyes were kept from recognizing him. And he said to them, 'What are you discussing with each other while you walk along?' They stood still, looking sad. Then one of them, whose name was Cleopas, answered him, 'Are you the only stranger in Jerusalem who does not know the things that have taken place there in these days?' He asked them, 'What things?' They replied, 'The things about Jesus of Nazareth, who was a prophet mighty in deed and word before God and all the people, and how our chief priests and leaders handed him over to be condemned to death and crucified him. But we *had hoped* that he was the one to redeem Israel.'[12]

---

[12] Luke 13:21–34 (NRSV).

'*We had hoped*', they say, but now we have lost that hope. However, Luke is the master of dramatic irony, for of course the stranger to whom they tell these things is the risen Christ who has triumphed over death. The very scriptures themselves are completely transfigured when they are read in the presence of and in conversation with Jesus, the Word of God.

> Then he said to them, 'Oh, how foolish you are, and how slow of heart to believe all that the prophets have declared! Was it not necessary that the Messiah should suffer these things and then enter into his glory?' Then beginning with Moses and all the prophets, he interpreted to them the things about himself in all the scriptures.[13]

Tantalisingly Luke doesn't tell us which passages, Jesus had expounded, but we have

[13] Luke 24:25–27 (NRSV).

SCRIPTURE: THE WORD BENEATH THE WORDS

not far to look, as the whole Bible is ringing and resounding with them.

> He was despised and rejected by others;
> a man of suffering and acquainted with infirmity;
> ... Surely he has borne our infirmities and carried our diseases;
> yet we accounted him stricken,
> struck down by God, and afflicted.
> But he was wounded for our transgressions,
> crushed for our iniquities;
> upon him was the punishment that made us whole.[14]

This, and so many other passages, fell on the infant Church with a force of revelation even though they had once been so familiar but never understood. I tried to imagine what this experience must have been like in my own poem:

---

[14] Isaiah 53:3–5 (NRSV).

Emmaus

We thought that everything was lost and
	gone,
Disaster on disaster overtook us
The night we left our Jesus all alone
And we were scattered, and our faith
	forsook us.
But oh that foul Friday proved far worse,
For we had hoped that he had been the one,
Till crucifixion proved he was a curse,
And on the cross our hopes were all
	undone.

Oh foolish heart why do you grieve?
Here is good news and comfort to your soul:
Open your mind to scripture and believe
He bore the curse for you to make you whole
The living God was numbered with the dead
That He might bring you Life in broken bread.[15]

---

[15] *Parable and Paradox*, Malcolm Guite (Canterbury Press, 2016), p. 77.

SCRIPTURE: THE WORD BENEATH THE WORDS

This brings us to a central point. We can speak of the scriptures as the 'Word of the Lord'. Properly speaking, Jesus Christ, himself, is the Word of the Lord, in the fullest sense of that term. But the words, the many words of scripture are vital, are still holy, precisely because they point to him, and they partake of his authority when, like those astonished disciples, we find Him in and through them.

And there is more. For through the faithful witness of the Gospel writers we can turn to Christ himself, we can ask him wider and deeper questions about how to interpret the scriptures. For these questions were indeed asked of him, and the most important question about the scriptures was this:

> 'Teacher, which is the greatest commandment in the Law?'
>
> Jesus replied: '"Love the Lord your God with all your heart and with all your soul and with all your mind." This is the first and greatest commandment. And the second is like it: "Love your neighbour as

yourself." All the Law and the Prophets hang on these two commandments.'[16]

Here, Christ himself gives us the interpretive key to the whole of the scriptures, and that key is *love*. St Augustine, in his little book *De Doctrina Christiana*[17], expresses beautifully what this means, having said that: 'we should clearly understand that the fulfillment and the end of the Law, and of all Holy Scripture, is ... love'.

St Augustine goes on to say:

> Whoever, then, thinks that he understands the Holy Scriptures, or any part of them, but puts such an interpretation upon them as does not tend to build up this twofold love of God and our neighbor, does not yet understand them as he ought. If, on the other hand, a man draws a meaning from them that may be used for the building up

---

[16] Matthew 22:34–40 (NRSV).
[17] *De doctrina Christiana* (On Christian Doctrine), St Augustine of Hippo, 397CE and 426CE.

of love, even though he does not happen upon the precise meaning which the author whom he reads intended to express in that place, his error is not pernicious, and he is wholly clear from the charge of deception. ... Whoever takes another meaning out of Scripture than the writer intended, goes astray, but not through any falsehood in Scripture. Nevertheless, as I was going to say, if his mistaken interpretation tends to build up love, which is the end of the commandment, he goes astray in much the same way as a man who by mistake quits the high road, but yet reaches through the fields the same place to which the road leads.[18]

How then should we read scripture? There is a place for study, for scholarship, for exposition, but the deepest way is meditation, is contemplating and reciting these scriptures in the presence of and in

[18] Translation from https://faculty.georgetown.edu/jod/augustine/ddc.html.

conversation with Christ. As St Paul says: 'Let the word of Christ dwell in you richly'.[19]

We need both the words, and the Word. We need the Word undergirding the words, the Word shimmering through the words. This is how I have approached the scriptures both as a believer and a poet.

Let me conclude this chapter with a story: when I was associate Vicar–Chaplain at St Edward's Cambridge, there was an elderly man who loved to read the scripture aloud from the King James Version in our services. You could see as he did it, how on each occasion, he was filled with awe at the privilege of reciting these holy words, these mysteries. My stall was just to the side and behind him as he stood at the lectern, and I remember watching his hands tremble above the page as he began to read. I wrote this poem, not only about how he read, but about how, when any of us reads the Bible, we discover how the Bible is reading us.

[19] Colossians 3:16 (NRSV).

The Lectern

Some rise on eagles wings, this one is plain,
Plain English workmanship in solid oak:
Age gracefully it says, *go with the grain*.
You walk towards an always open book,
Open as every life to every light,
Open to shade and shadow, day and night,
The changeless witness of your changing pain.
Be still the lectern says, *stand here and read*
Here are your mysteries, your love and fear,
And, running through them all, the slender thread
Of God's strange grace, red as these ribbons, red
As your own blood when reading reads you here
And pierces joint and marrow ... So you stand
The lectern still beneath your trembling hand. [20]

---

[20] 'The Lectern' from *Sounding the Seasons – Seventy Sonnets for the Christian Year*, Malcolm Guite (Canterbury Press, 2012), p. 2.

2
Liturgy: The Word
between the words

I ENDED MY chapter on Scripture with my poem about hearing the Bible read in Church, read out loud, as part of the shaped poem, the ritual and mutually enacted exchange of meaning, which is the Church's liturgy.

The word *liturgy* comes from ancient Greek (Greek: λειτουργία – *leitourgia*) which literally means *work of the people*. Though it means rather more than that: the element *litos* certainly means the people, the gathered congregation and is where we get the word laity from. But the element *ergos*, in liturgy, means rather more than just work, it suggests movement, action and energy. The liturgy is not simply an exchange of words but, through those words, the exchange and flow of meaning, not just abstract meaning, but meaning incarnate and embedded in beautiful language, language which is itself energised and transfigured every time it is used.

Why is liturgy important for me in sharing 'my theology'? Because liturgy doesn't just form and inform theology, it is where theology happens, where it is enacted, celebrated and assimilated – prayer is the school of theology. I can learn from the Bible for example, the theological truth that God 'was in Christ reconciling the World to himself,'[21] and that he has entrusted to us a ministry of reconciliation.[22] But that remains a paper truth, a mere intellectual assertion in my head, until in the midst of my busy life and gathered in the congregation with my neighbours I hear the proclamation of the Peace at the Eucharist. Christ's Peace is offered afresh as my neighbours and I exchange the words of that Peace and through our gestures turn it from a proposition into an action. Then, and only then, is the potential energy of truth actualised and exchanged.

In the next chapter I will touch on the deepest gift and mystery of all liturgies: the

[21] 2 Corinthians 5:19 (NRSV).
[22] 2 Corinthians 5:11–20 (NRSV).

Eucharist. But first I want to talk about liturgy more widely and touch on the importance of the liturgical year. For this bodying forth of abstract truth into the actualities of everyday life is not only found in the ritual repetition of a set liturgy but also, in its carefully organised seasonal variety. Thanks to the wonderful invention of the liturgical year, as essential to the movement and dynamics of liturgy as the invention of the wheel was to transport, the participant in liturgy finds the whole salvation story in all its theological depth, enacted and played out through the changing seasons of their own life. For example: the academic student of theology studies the doctrine of the Trinity as a specialist subject, with its own peculiar history and technical terminology, but, for the Christian partaking of the liturgy, it is a dynamic exchange of love woven through the year. There are times when the liturgical season focusses on one person of the Trinity, when it glories in the Father as creator, and the Son as redeemer, when in the season of

Pentecost, it delights in the Spirit, as the one who breathes through the creation, the scripture and the liturgy itself, takes up our own brief prayers and hopes and makes them part of the very exchange of love between the Father and the Son. But there are also special occasions in the liturgical year when we focus on the whole Trinity. So, for example, there is a day when we remember the Baptism of Jesus, and see unveiled for a moment in the Gospel, the Father delighting in the Son, the Son offering himself in full obedience to the Father and the Spirit himself, descending as a dove to fill and bless Jesus and us in him. In the poem for this particular Sunday, in *Sounding the Seasons,*[23] my cycle of sonnets for the liturgical year, I tried to express something of what that moment in scripture means, when it is lifted off the cold page and kindled afresh in the life of the Church:

---

[23] *Sounding the Seasons, Seventy Sonnets for the Christian Year*, Malcolm Guite (Canterbury Press, 2012).

LITURGY: THE WORD BETWEEN THE WORDS

The Baptism of Christ

Beginning here we glimpse the Three-in-one;
The river runs, the clouds are torn apart,
The Father speaks, the Spirit and the Son
Reveal to us the single loving heart
That beats behind the being of all things
And calls and keeps and kindles us to light.
The dove descends, the spirit soars and sings
'You are belovèd, you are my delight!'
In that swift light and life, as water spills
And streams around the Man like quickening rain,
The voice that made the universe reveals
The God in Man who makes it new again.
He calls us too, to step into that river,
To die and rise and live and love forever.[24]

---

[24] *Sounding the Seasons, Seventy Sonnets for the Christian Year*, Malcolm Guite (Canterbury Press, 2012), p. 20.

A little later in the year, the liturgy brings us Trinity Sunday and often the readings ask us not only to consider God as Trinity but also to see ourselves as made in the image of Trinity, made *by* a communion and communication of love *for* a communion and communication of love, made by a Triune Poet that, together, we might make poetry of our own lives. Again, this is something I could draw out more fully in poetry than in prose:

Trinity Sunday

In the Beginning, not in time or space,
But in the quick before both space and
    time,
In Life, in Love, in co–inherent Grace,
In three in one and one in three, in rhyme,
In music, in the whole creation story,
In His own image, His imagination,
The Triune Poet makes us for His glory,
And makes us each the other's
    inspiration.
He calls us out of darkness, chaos,
    chance,
To improvise a music of our own,

LITURGY: THE WORD BETWEEN THE WORDS

> To sing the chord that calls us to the dance,
> Three notes resounding from a single tone,
> To sing the End in whom we all begin;
> Our God beyond, beside us, and within.[25]

In some ways, these reflections on liturgy are a natural continuation of what I had said about scripture in the previous chapter. To speak of liturgy is really to speak of scripture in another mode. For the most part all the great liturgies of the church are made up from loved and remembered passages of scripture, but this time it is no longer scripture flat on the page, but scripture that has been invited to get up and dance, to move us and to move with us. We read it, and chant it antiphonally, it flows back and forth from one side of the Church to the other, back and forth between the congregation and clergy, back and forth between our heads and our hearts. This way

[25] *Sounding the Seasons, Seventy Sonnets for the Christian Year*, Malcolm Guite (Canterbury Press, 2012), p. 48.

of animating scripture has its roots not only in the early Church, but in the monasteries and, supremely, in the Benedictine Tradition. As a medieval Cistercian once wrote, advising monks how to read scripture:

> The Holy Scripture is the well of Jacob from which the waters are drawn which will be poured out later in prayer. Thus, there will be no need to go to the oratory to begin to pray; but in reading itself, means will be found for prayer and contemplation.[26]

Of all the scriptures to be drawn out of that well, and poured out later in prayer, surely the Book of Psalms is the greatest, for these scriptures were already prayer and song, were already liturgy before they were scripture. When we chant the Psalms we are praying prayers that were on the lips of Christ, and participating in a tradition which goes back centuries before Christianity, which we share

[26] Arnoul of Boheriss quoted by Jean LeClercq OSB, *The Love of Learning and the Desire for God* (SPCK, 1978), p. 90.

LITURGY: THE WORD BETWEEN THE WORDS

with the ancient and living faith of the Jewish peoples.

The Psalms are ancient, and yet always new, as I found when I prayed them afresh as part of the daily offices during the course of the pandemic and lockdowns of 2020. As I wrote in the Preface to *David's Crown*, the collection of new poetry I composed in response to these ancient poems:

> Like many people, I have found that the experience of crisis and darkness through which we are presently living has brought my reading of Scripture to life and especially my engagement with the Psalter. Familiar words, recited by rote, have suddenly taken on power and resonance: pleas for help and mercy, confessions of despair, longings for renewal, thanksgivings for recovery, heartfelt cries for justice; all these passages in psalms which we may have recited almost absentmindedly in happier years have become once more what they were always intended to be – the direct speech of the

heart. And in this we are not making a new discovery but returning to a great tradition.[27]

Why are the Psalms such a key to the nature of liturgy itself, why are they so enduring, so sustaining? Perhaps because they contain and express so much pain and suffering, and yet begin and end with praise and blessing. The word Psalm means praise, and the Book of Psalms is really the Book of Praises. The first Psalm *Beatus Vir* begins with a beatitude, a blessing 'Blessed is the man ...' and forms a portal or invitation into the whole book and, indeed, into liturgy itself. I tried to capture something of this in my own poem on that Psalm, the opening poem in *David's Crown*:

Beatus vir qui non abiit

Come to the place where every breath is
    praise,
And God is breathing through each
    passing breeze.

[27] *David's Crown*, Malcolm Guite (Canterbury Press, 2021), p. 1.

LITURGY: THE WORD BETWEEN THE WORDS

Be planted by the waterside and raise

Your arms with Christ beneath these
    rooted trees,
Who lift their breathing leaves up to the
    skies.
Be rooted too, as still and strong as these,

Open alike to sun and rain. Arise
From meditation by these waters. Bear
The fruit of that deep rootedness. Be wise

In the trees' long wisdom. Learn to share
The secret of their patience. Pass the day
In their green fastness and their quiet air.

Slowly discern a life, a truth, a way,
Where simple being flowers in delight.
Then let the chaff of life just blow away.[28]

---

[28] *David's Crown*, Malcolm Guite (Canterbury Press, 2021), p. 1.

The Psalms, unsurprisingly, were right at the heart of the Benedictine life and the monks recited the whole Psalter every week, as its individual poems were distributed and sung antiphonally throughout their daily offices. Those Benedictine offices eventually gave rise, in the Church of England, to the traditions of Morning and Evening Prayer with their regular allotment of psalms. Of those two offices it is Evening Prayer or Evensong, as it has come to be known, that has been most formative for me. This is partly because I have had the honour of being a Chaplain at a Cambridge College at which Evensong, according to the BCP, with its set Psalms in Coverdale's,[29] translation has been sung beautifully by our Choir.

As a piece of liturgical shaping, Evensong is a work of genius. At the beginning of each academic year I try to give new students some sense of the richness and depth of the tradition on which they are entering, by showing them how the liturgy is shaped to make them

---

[29] Myles or Miles Coverdale (1488 – 1569), an English church reformer and Bible translator.

LITURGY: THE WORD BETWEEN THE WORDS

participants in the salvation story, to take them on a journey. The key to understanding this, is to understand the context in the Bible of all those passages out of which Cranmer has allusively created the new 'collage-poem' of Evensong. So when the cantor sings *Oh Lord open thou our lips* and they respond *and our mouth shall show forth they praise* they should know these words are from Psalm 51. For a moment we have become King David, recovering from the agony of his guilt over Bathsheba and trying to begin again with God, and this is apt for this moment in the liturgy, because we too have just confessed our sins and received their absolution. Now, as sinful and as forgiven as David was, we are ready to join with him in singing his Psalms and that is the next thing that happens in Evensong. It is only after the Psalms have been sung that we hear our first reading from the Old Testament, for in this liturgy we do not read flat and unprepared but rather we sing ourselves into scripture. The rest of Evensong is shaped so as to give us a full sense of the meaning of the transition from the Old to the New Testament, to help us to understand how the two Testaments are related, how the one mediates the other. For between the Old and the New Testament readings comes the *Magnificat*[30], the revolutionary song of Mary. For Mary mediates between the two Testaments: she inherits the promises of the Old and brings to birth the promise of the New. Even as we sing with her that 'all generations shall call me blessed' we realise that we ourselves, in singing those words, are a fulfilment of that scripture, as we bless her in song. Then, at last, we are ready to receive the New Testament, the Testament made possible by Mary's fruitful obedience. We receive it very much as Simeon received and recognised the Christ–child when Mary brought him into the Temple and so, in a moment of poetic genius, Cranmer gives us Simeon's Song as our response and we sing the *Nunc Dimittis*.[31] Two passages from Luke's Gospel have been lifted off the page to come

---

[30] *The Magnificat*: Luke 1:46–55 (KJV).
[31] *Nunc Dimittis*: Luke 2:29–3 (KJV).

alive in a new way within us. The Liturgy invites us first to become the young girl singing her song of triumph and then to become the old man who has come to know peace at last. We take these insights and experiences with us outside and beyond the liturgy into the world. None of us knows when our end will come, but the liturgy makes us ready for it, as for all things, and in the *Nunc Dimittis* we have already been given all the last words we will ever need:

> Lord, now lettest thou thy servant depart
>   in peace according to thy word.
> For mine eyes have seen thy salvation,
> Which thou hast prepared before the face
>   of all people;
> To be a light to lighten the Gentiles and to
>   be the glory of thy people Israel.[32]

---

[32] *Nunc Dimittis*, Book of Common Prayer, 1662 / Luke 2:29–3 KJV

3

Sacrament: The Word transforms the world

IN THE LAST chapter I tried to give a sense of how 'my theology' is formed by the services of Morning and Evening Prayer, by 'The Liturgy of the Word'. But these non-eucharistic services are always and only a kind of preparation, an outer vestibule for the true heart of Christian liturgy which is the Eucharist itself. For even though the Word himself underpins and gives meaning to all words, and can come to us glimmering through the words of scripture and liturgy, as his spirit breathes on them and kindles them afresh in our hearts, there is nevertheless a danger that we stop at the words themselves, that we mistake the *signs* for the *mystery* to which they point, and so miss the mystery altogether. For there is always a mystery that transcends the very language with which we try to capture it. As C. S. Lewis says in his telling little poem *An Apologist's Evening Prayer*:

> Thoughts are but coins. Let me not trust, instead
> Of Thee, their thin-worn image of Thy head.[33]

Indeed, the poet Edwin Muir takes that even further, in his poem *The Incarnate One* and recalls how sometimes church culture can degenerate into such wordy legalism that it misses the mystery altogether, as he puts it bleakly:

> The Word made flesh is here made word again ...
> the mystery is impaled and bent
> Into an ideological argument [34]

It is as though Jesus knew that we might flee the intimate proximity of Incarnation, and reduce it again to our own discourse, and so made provision at the heart of Christian

---

[33] *Poems* – a collection of C. S. Lewis's poems edited by Walter Hooper (Geoffrey Bles, 1964).
[34] *Prometheus*, Edwin Muir (Faber & Faber, 1954).

worship for the sacrament of his bodily presence in an act that begins with words but goes far beyond them. In this way those amongst us for whom words come too easily are humbled and silenced, and those for whom language is difficult or impossible are fed and nourished.

But if I am to tell you what the sacrament means to me and how completely it has formed not just 'my theology' but my very identity, then I must tell you a personal story:

I was an atheist when I came up to Cambridge as an undergraduate in 1977, having firmly and fully rejected the Christian faith in which I had been brought up. At first, I sought to replace it with a completely reductive 'scientific' account of the world, trying to persuade myself that all the mysteries of our humanity might be reduced to biochemistry. Though by the time I arrived at Cambridge I had begun to be sceptical of my scepticism. The depth and power of my personal experience of poetry must be more, I began to realise, than the unwinding of enzymes and the outworking of selfish genes. So I was, I suppose, an atheist gradually becoming an agnostic. At Cambridge I fell in love with medieval literature and began, by way of research, to read some of the great theology that lay behind it, particularly St Augustine. I was deeply impressed, and began to see that there was rather more to Christianity than moralising sermons and church jumble sales. I still didn't think that it was really true, that there was *actually* a God, but I began to tell myself that it was, perhaps, *psychologically* true, that it made some kind of inner, personal sense even if it, sadly, wasn't actually the case.

Then one day, in the summer of 1979, I was reading the Book of Psalms, again as part of the 'background' for medieval poetry. I was completely alone in an empty house in Ealing. Suddenly, reading Psalm 145, with the Bible open in my hand, I had an overwhelming awareness of God's presence. Perhaps it was triggered by those verses:

SACRAMENT: THE WORD TRANSFORMS THE WORLD

> The Lord is nigh unto all them that call
> upon him,
> to all that call upon him in truth.[35]

But the truth was, that I wasn't calling upon him! I was reading aloud a poem addressed to him, safe in the naïve assumption that he wasn't there. But he was! Suddenly he disclosed his presence. Many people read Psalm 145 for comfort:

> The Lord upholdeth all that fall,
> and raiseth up all those that be bowed
> down.[36]

But my sudden sense of God's overwhelming presence was not comforting at all – it was alarming! It is hard to put it into words. At one moment I was at the centre of the room, the centre of my life, the centre of that circle in which we all find ourselves naturally when we open our eyes look around: for we occupy

---

[35] Psalm 145:18 (KJV).
[36] Psalm 145:14 (KJV).

the middle and the World extends in widening circles around us. And the next moment I was not in the centre at all. I was on the very furthest of edges, hanging over the abyss by a mere thread, for the centre was now fully occupied by the only One who could ever be there. This ineluctable, inexpressible, all-holy Presence filled the room, and compared with him I now saw everything else as tangential, contingent, dependent. Much later I came across the famous passage in Isaiah:

> In the year that King Uzziah died, I saw the Lord sitting on a throne, high and lofty; and the hem of his robe filled the temple.[37]

Now when Isaiah had that experience he didn't say 'this is wonderful, I have just had a religious experience, I must be a holy person, I will go and start a cult in California' on the contrary, he says:

---

[37] Isaiah 6:1 (NRSV).

SACRAMENT: THE WORD TRANSFORMS THE WORLD

'... Woe is me! I am lost, for I am a man of unclean lips, and I live among a people of unclean lips; yet my eyes have seen the King, the Lord of hosts!'[38]

That was exactly my experience, I absolutely knew that God was there, but I didn't feel that I belonged nor could I dare to turn and face him. And this was not a fleeting experience, it was constant. After a day or two of hoping to wake up and find that this 'episode' was over, I realised that God wasn't going to go away. Not knowing what else to do, I contacted my College Chaplain – you have to be desperate to do that – he was a wonderful listener and suggested I return to College early and then invited me to join him daily in saying the Psalms at Morning and Evening Prayer. His reasoning was that since the Psalms had initiated the experience, and my mistake, indeed my sin, had been to read them as mere literature,

---

[38] Isaiah 6:5 (NRSV).

as though God was not there, then the only thing I could reasonably do was to read them again, but this time fully and frankly addressing them to that ineluctable presence. But he added an interesting and, it turned out, insightful stipulation, 'You must say the Psalms with me, but I forbid you to say the *Gloria* with me at the end of them. You have some sense of the Father, but as yet you know nothing of the Son or the Holy Spirit and you should not take their names in vain.'

He was right, and I found those mornings and evenings in Chapel were the one time in the day when I could indeed dare to face the One who was still there in the centre, in all his unapproachable holiness. I could turn to him and praise him with the words of this 'book of praises' and it was at first an immense relief and then a growing joy to do so.

Then towards the end of that Michaelmas Term, I went to hear Eric Doyle, one of the great contemporary Franciscan Friars, preaching in Cambridge. Again I believed I was attending for 'research' purposes. The Franciscan influence is all over medieval literature and I thought it would deepen my understanding if I listened to a Franciscan preacher myself. Eric Doyle was giving a series of three addresses on the blessed sacrament and near the beginning of the first address, he suddenly spoke movingly about 'not being at the centre', about being 'utterly dependent'.

He gave the example of a babe in the womb, entirely dependent on the sustaining and loving presence of its mother and all that comes through the umbilical cord. And then of the newborn babe uttering its first cry:

> 'All it can do is cry, it cannot even turn itself over or move itself for light and food, everything still depends on the sustaining presence and love of a mother.'

Oh how I recognised that experience!

'I know what you are thinking', he continued, 'you are thinking that is how we are with God, that holy presence at the centre of all things, who makes and sustains all things. We hang on the edges of that love and presence, utterly dependent for everything on him. In one sense that is true, but that is not what I have come to tell you. For the astonishing paradox, the utterly unexpected Good News of the Gospel is that it is God himself who has become the little babe, God who was dependent in the womb at the end of the umbilical cord. God, before whom, in one sense, we are weak and dependent, nevertheless chooses to come to us in utter weakness and dependence. He, who has no need, comes to us in complete need, comes to us in utter vulnerability. Lest he should overwhelm us, he becomes one of us. That baby in the manger could do nothing for himself, all he could do was cry and depend completely on the loving provision of Mary and Joseph.'

Somehow, as Eric Doyle was saying these things, the penny dropped, something utterly changed in me. It is not that I lost the sense of that holy, luminous presence, if anything it grew, but, perhaps for the first time in my

SACRAMENT: THE WORD TRANSFORMS THE WORLD

life, I felt that it was all right to be human, that this God from whom I felt so much on the *outside* was also *inside*, that he knew my humanity from within. Suddenly I understood that God the Father was also God the Son, and that God the Spirit had filled Mary and sown the Son in her womb. I knew that I was ready to go back to my Chaplain and to say that *Gloria*!

But Eric Doyle wasn't quite finished, for he went on to speak of the Sacrament:

> 'and if the babe in the manger came to us in helplessness, that he might approach us with no overwhelming or overshadowing, no threats or domination, then how much more helpless is Christ when he comes to us in bread and wine. This little wafer cannot even cry, it is utterly vulnerable in your hands, you might fling him away and tread him underfoot but he comes to you in loving hope that you will receive him.'

I became a Christian that day and have been one ever since.

So you will see why the sacrament of Communion is so central for me, and why, in one sense the foundation of this sacrament for me is always the Incarnation, of which it is an expression and continuation. Many years after that moment of conversion and my long and nourishing experience of regularly receiving the sacrament, I wrote this poem about that communion:

Love's Choice

This bread is light, dissolving, almost air,
A little visitation on my tongue,
A wafer–thin sensation, hardly there.
This taste of wine is brief in flavour, flung
A moment to the palate's roof and fled,
Even its aftertaste a memory.
Yet this is how he comes. Through wine
    and bread
Love chooses to be emptied into me.
He does not come in unimagined light
Too bright to be denied, too absolute

SACRAMENT: THE WORD TRANSFORMS THE WORLD

For consciousness, too strong for sight,
Leaving the seer blind, the poet mute;
Chooses instead to seep into each sense,
To dye himself into experience.[39]

In all the years of communion since then, I have come to understand that it is not just the Incarnation but also the Passion and the Resurrection which are actualised and made part of our own flesh and blood in this sacrament. In one sense, I had already hinted that in the last line of this sonnet with its play on the word 'dye'. That hint was deepened and confirmed over the years in which I first heard, and then later as a priest myself, prayed the Prayer of Consecration, in which I thanked God for that tender mercy in which 'He gave his only son Jesus Christ to suffer death upon the cross for our own redemption.' The Passion was already implicit in the Incarnation, the Prayer of Consecration makes it explicit. The

[39] *Sounding the Seasons, Seventy Sonnets for the Christian Year*, Malcolm Guite (Canterbury Press, 2012) pp. 49.

pure change that happens at the moment of consecration is also the pure change that happens for all of us, because of the crucifixion. I tried to get some sense of it in the eleventh of my series of poems on the Stations of the Cross:

XI Crucifixion: Jesus is nailed to the cross

See, as they strip the robe from off his back
And spread his arms and nail them to the
 cross,
The dark nails pierce him and the sky turns
 black,
And love is firmly fastened onto loss.
But here a pure change happens. On this tree
Loss becomes gain, death opens into birth.
Here wounding heals and fastening makes
 free,
Earth breathes in heaven, heaven roots in \
 earth.
And here we see the length, the breadth,
 the height,
Where love and hatred meet and love stays
 true,

SACRAMENT: THE WORD TRANSFORMS THE WORLD

> Where sin meets grace and darkness turns to light,
> We see what love can bear and be and do.
> And here our Saviour calls us to his side,
> His love is free, his arms are open wide.[40]

The Eucharist is not only my continuous personal encounter with all Christ has done for me in his Death and Resurrection, it is also a communion with the whole church, with all the saints living and departed 'with all stand before you in earth and heaven'. Here the veil between the worlds is not simply thinner, but like the veil in the temple at the moment of Jesus' death, it is torn in two from top to bottom! Because God is in Christ reconciling the world to himself, I no longer need that protecting veil between me and the 'holy of holies': for 'we have a great high priest, that is passed into the heavens, Jesus the Son of God'. [41]

---

[40] *Sounding the Seasons, Seventy Sonnets for the Christian Year*, Malcolm Guite (Canterbury Press, 2012), pp. 42.
[41] Hebrews 4:14 (KJV).

Perhaps it is only poetry that can help us apprehend something of the mystery and paradox of this central action of the Church. Of all the poets who have responded to the Eucharist, it is George Herbert who continues to move me most, not only in the beautiful ending of his poem *The Agony*:

> Love is that liquor sweet and most divine
> Which my God feels as blood but I as wine[42]

But supremely, in *Love III,* the closing poem of *The Temple*, a poem which is itself an inner commentary on Herbert's experience of the Book of Common Prayer Communion Service:

> LOVE bade me welcome; yet my soul drew back,
> Guilty of dust and sin.
> But quick–eyed Love, observing me grow slack

---

[42] 'The Agony (*or The Agonie*)', *The Temple*, George Herbert (1633).

SACRAMENT: THE WORD TRANSFORMS THE WORLD

From my first entrance in,
Drew nearer to me, sweetly questioning
If I lack'd anything.

'A guest,' I answer'd, 'worthy to be here:'
Love said, 'You shall be he.'
'I, the unkind, ungrateful? Ah, my dear,
I cannot look on Thee.'
Love took my hand and smiling did
    reply,
'Who made the eyes but I?'

'Truth, Lord; but I have marr'd them: let my
    shame
Go where it doth deserve.'
'And know you not,' says Love, 'Who bore
    the blame?'
'My dear, then I will serve.'
'You must sit down,' says Love, 'and taste
    my meat.'
So I did sit and eat.[43]

---

[43] 'Love (III)', *The Temple*, George Herbert (1633).

It is wonderful how delicately the courteous minuet of approaching and retiring, of confidence and hesitation and finally of full welcome, reflects the movement of the Communion Service itself. For the same delicate dance is there in that Service, from the Collect for Purity with its mention of our known desires and unhidden secrets, through to the Confession and Absolution and then the assurance of the Comfortable Words, until we have a last hesitation in the Prayer of Humble Access and finally the resolution of the Communion itself.

At the end of that Service we are sent back into the World with a Blessing, and this is, perhaps, the most important thing of all. The Sacrament we celebrate in Church is a training of the eye, a cleansing of the doors of perception, as William Blake put it [44]. For having learned to discern the full presence of Christ in Bread and Wine and taken that presence into ourselves, we must learn to discern the

---

[44] *The Marriage of Heaven and Hell*, William Blake (1793).

presence of Christ in the World, especially in all the people we meet, for Christ tells us that whatever we do for the least of them we do for him.

Conclusion: Christ alive and loose in the world

EVERYTHING I HAVE said so far, in my account of scripture, liturgy and sacrament, is no more than the womb or cradle in which my faith, 'my theology' has been formed and nurtured. But now I want to tell you what that faith and theology are like when they are born and living, when they are let loose into the world. For otherwise I might be giving a very false impression – the idea that God is to be found only within three feet of an open Bible or at the altar rail of a parish church. Of course, God is to be found there – the Liturgy and Sacraments of the Church are among his covenanted graces – for God has indeed covenanted to meet us in his Holy Scriptures, where we read them in his spirit, and in bread and wine, where his Holy Spirit transforms them and us as we make our communion. But it is not *only* there that he meets us, and we are not the *only* people whom he meets. The God whom we meet in Jesus, crucified and risen, is also the God of the Cosmos:

> He is the image of the invisible God, the firstborn of all creation; for in him all things in heaven and on earth were created, things visible and invisible, whether thrones or dominions or rulers or powers—all things have been created through him and for him. He himself is before all things, and in him all things hold together.[45]

This passage is totally inclusive. The phrase '*all things*' sounds through it like a summoning chorus: '*all things* created through him'; 'he is before *all things*' – that is he founds, undergirds and strains them – 'in him *all things*

---

[45] Colossians 1:15–17 (NRSV).

CONCLUSION: CHRIST ALIVE AND LOOSE IN THE WORLD

hold together'. The God to whom these verses point, the God whom we praise in liturgy and receive in sacrament, is not to be contained in a box, however spacious or architecturally distinguished. As we said at the end of the last chapter, participation in liturgy, and sacrament is a training of the eye, so that on leaving church we are ready to recognise Christ anywhere and everywhere. I tried to put it like this in a poem once:

A Lens

Not that we think he is confined to us,
Locked in the box of our religious rites,
Or curtained by these frail cathedral walls,
No church is broad or creed compendious
Enough. All thought's a narrowing of sites,
Before him every definition fails,
Words fall and flutter into emptiness,
Like motes of dust within his spaciousness.

Not that we summon him, but that he lends
The very means whereby he might be known,
Till this opacity of stone on stone,

> This trace of light and music on the air,
> This sacred space itself becomes a lens
> To sense his presence who is everywhere.[46]

In one sense the thought in that poem is entirely mine, part of 'my theology', but in another sense it is part of the traditional teaching I have received. In fact, the core idea probably came to me from C. S. Lewis, appropriately enough in his *Letters to Malcolm*:

> … if these holy places, things, and days cease to remind us, if they obliterate our awareness that all ground is holy and every bush (could we but perceive it) a Burning Bush, then the hallows begin to do us harm. [47]

Indeed a little after that passage, Lewis draws our attention to what one might call a sacrament of the present moment. Our

---

[46] *After Prayer*, Malcolm Guite (Canterbury Press, 2019), pp. 71.
[47] *Letters to Malcolm: Chiefly on Prayer*, C. S. Lewis (Geoffrey Bles, 1964), p. 100. Copyright C. S. Lewis 1963, 1964.

CONCLUSION: CHRIST ALIVE AND LOOSE IN THE WORLD

present situation, wherever we are, is 'at every moment, a possible theophany. Here is the holy ground; the Bush is burning now'.[48] And this is to say much more than even Coleridge was saying in *Frost at Midnight*. In that great passage, in which he recognised that nature is not only a collection of things, a set of physical phenomena, but also a kind of language, a poem, words spoken to us by the Word himself:

> The lovely shapes and sounds intelligible
> Of that eternal language, which thy God
> Utters, who from eternity doth teach
> Himself in all, and all things in himself.
> Great universal Teacher! he shall mould
> Thy spirit, and by giving make it ask. [49]

Coleridge is right to speak of nature as God's language, but if we want to know what God is

---

[48] *Letters to Malcolm: Chiefly on Prayer*, C. S. Lewis (Geoffrey Bles, 1964), p. 109. Copyright C. S. Lewis 1963, 1964.

[49] S. T. Coleridge: *Poetical Works Part 1*, poem 171, 'Frost at Midnight', pp. 452–6, lines 54–64.

actually saying to us in that language, if we want a key to interpret the divine poem, then we must look to the pattern of Christ, not just to the Word behind the world, but to the Word made flesh. Not just to the Word crucified but to the Word, risen, alive and at large.

The Resurrection of Jesus Christ is not only the climax of the Gospels, it is the turning point of the cosmos, the singularity, the explosion of love out of which the new creation begins to unfold even in the midst of the old. It is the definitive breaking open of any 'religious box' in which we thought we might contain God, or even the story of Jesus. Because Jesus is alive, and free, the story of Jesus himself is not over, it is still unfolding. Just as he had compassion for the poor and the wounded in the Gospel stories, came close to them and healed them, he continues to do so now. He is alive and at large, he is sharing his love well beyond the confines of those churches where he has, nevertheless, promised to meet us. I rediscovered this in a powerful way during the course of the first lockdown in the Spring of 2020. It will be clear from this book that Communion is vital to me, it is where I delight to meet Christ and am assured of how he nurtures and sustains me. So, like so many of us, I was deeply troubled to find our Churches locked on Easter Day, the day when, supremely one wants to make one's communion. But looking back now I find this deprivation was salutary, for it forced me to look beyond the church, to all the places and people, where the free and risen Christ is to be found *outside* the Church. In the early hours of that strange Easter Day I composed a poem which, perhaps, embodies 'my theology', my Christian hope more fully than anything else I have ever written, and it seems the right poem with which to conclude this little book:

Easter 2020

And where is Jesus, this strange Easter day?
Not lost in our locked churches, anymore
Than he was sealed in that dark sepulchre.

MY THEOLOGY — MALCOLM GUITE

The locks are loosed; the stone is rolled away,
And he is up and risen, long before,
Alive, at large, and making his strong way
Into the world he gave his life to save,
No need to seek him in his empty grave.

He might have been a wafer in the hands
Of priests this day, or music from the lips
Of red–robed choristers, instead he slips
Away from church, shakes off our linen bands
To don his apron with a nurse: he grips
And lifts a stretcher, soothes with gentle hands
The frail flesh of the dying, gives them hope,
Breathes with the breathless, lends them strength to cope.

On Thursday we applauded, for he came
And served us in a thousand names and faces
Mopping our sickroom floors and catching traces

CONCLUSION: CHRIST ALIVE AND LOOSE IN THE WORLD

Of that *corona* which was death to him:
Good Friday happened in a thousand places
Where Jesus held the helpless, died with them
That they might share his Easter in their need,
Now they are risen with him, risen indeed.[50]

---

[50] This poem will be included in one of my forthcoming collections, but has already been included in Tom Wright's book *God and the Pandemic* (SPCK, 2020).

Also available:

MY THEOLOGY
ROBERT BECKFORD
DUPPY CONQUEROR

'How can people racialised as black conceive God, Jesus, and the Spirit within contemporary concrete social and political worlds?' asks pioneering black theologian and broadcaster Robert Beckford. 'What would facilitate a radical theology committed to confronting racialised injustice, social inequality and environmental degradation?'

In *Duppy Conqueror* Beckford explains how he has recontextualised African-American black and womanist theologies of liberation to answer these questions for second and third-generation black British. His methodologies have included a correlation of linguistic concepts from black cultural history and urban life with theological concepts, and the inscription of black theology onto documentary filmmaking and contemporary gospel music.

Also available:

MY THEOLOGY
ILIA DELIO
THE PRIMACY OF LOVE

'What do we live for? This is the question many of us ask at the end of a very long day, especially in the conflicted moments of life,' writes Ilia Delio. 'My answer is simple: we live to love. If we doubt love, we doubt our own existence.'

In this compelling book Delio explores the metaphysics of love at the centre of her theological thinking. From the cosmological to the theological dimensions of existence, she shows love to be the irresistible force of attraction that leads straight into the heart of God.

Also available:

M Y T H E O L O G Y
ALISTER McGRATH
RETURN FROM A DISTANT COUNTRY

'I never expected to be a Christian theologian, mainly because I never expected to be a Christian,' writes Alister McGrath. 'I assumed that scientific atheism would be my permanent intellectual homeland; in fact, it turned out to be a temporary place of exile, from which I would later return, wiser and somewhat chastened.'

In this fascinating book, McGrath describes his journey into faith and his vision of Christian theology, focussing on the distinct role of historical theology; the importance of engaging the relation of science and faith; the need for theologians to engage in major public debates; and the significance of theological education.

MY THEOLOGY

The world's leading Christian thinkers explain some of the principal tenets of their theological beliefs.

Collect the full library.

September 2021

1. Robert Beckford
2. Ilia Delio
3. Malcolm Guite
4. Alister McGrath

November 2021

5. Guy Consolmagno
6. Ann Loades
7. Rachel Mann
8. Keith Ward

January 2022

9. Cynthia Bourgeault
10. Grace Ji-Sun Kim
11. John Swinton
12. Mpho Tutu van Furth

March 2022

13. Joan Chittister
14. Shane Clifton
15. Scot McKnight
16. Siku